Projects Inspired by Neighbourhoods

Julie Ashfield, Rebecca Bruce, Sarah Deas,

Nigel Meager, Peter Newbury, Noel Springett-McHugh,

Stephen Springe... ...**Claire van Rhyn**

Acknowledgements

Julie Ashfield (Chapter 5) would like to thank the staff and pupils at Peterston Super Ely C/W Primary, Vale of Glamorgan for their wonderful work.

Rebecca Bruce (Chapter 7) would like to thank the children and staff at Slade Primary School, Tonbridge, especially Nicola Hill, Sheena Soweby, Diana Faunce and Vivienne Resch. Thanks also to Hilden Grange School.

Sarah Deas (Chapter 2) would like to thank all the Reception children at John Betts and to Mary Caveney and Emma Condon for all their support and enthusiasm.

Nigel Meager (Chapter 6) would like to thank Head Teacher Mr Richard Endall and all the staff and children at Winterton Primary School and Nursery, Norfolk.

Peter Newbury (Chapter 8) would like to thank everyone involved at Walwayne Court Primary School, Trowbridge.

Claire van Rhyn (Chapters 1 and 3) would like to thank the children and teachers of Barnes Primary School, in particular Mrs Grant, Mrs Leissle, Mr O'Donnell, Mr Brian, Ms Baxter and Ms Ducker, Mrs Garofalo, Mrs Wilson and their classes of 2011–12.

Noel Springett-McHugh (Chapter 4) would like to say thank you to Ms Reynolds and the Year Four children at Southend Junior School.

Stephen Springett-McHugh (Chapter 4) would like to thank head teacher Andrea Curtis and all the staff and governors at Bushfield School.

Published by Collins
An imprint of HarperCollins*Publishers*
77–85 Fulham Palace Road
Hammersmith
London
W6 8JB

© HarperCollins*Publishers* Limited 2013

10 9 8 7 6 5 4 3 2 1

ISBN-13 978 0 00 748699 1

Julie Ashfield, Rebecca Bruce, Sarah Deas, Nigel Meager, Peter Newbury, Noel Springett-McHugh, Stephen Springett-McHugh and Claire van Rhyn assert their moral rights to be identified as authors of this work.

British Library Cataloguing in Publication Data
A Catalogue record for this publication is available from the British Library

Cover and internal design by Steve Evans Design and Illustration
Edited by Alison Sage and Gaby Frescura
Proofread by Ros and Chris Davies
Photography by Arted EU Limited and Elmcroft Studios

Printed and bound by Printing Express Limited, Hong Kong

Browse the complete Collins catalogue at
www.collinseducation.com

MIX
Paper from responsible sources
FSC
www.fsc.org
FSC C007454

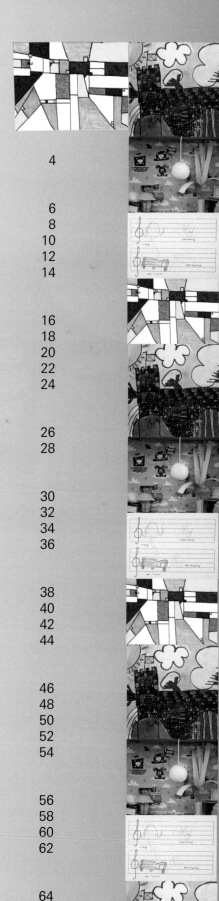

Contents

Introduction 4

Where Do I Live?
Global neighbours 6
Photographic community portraits 8
Mapping community networks 10
My town, your town 12
My ideal space 14

What Is My School Like?
Sounds around our school 16
Shapes in our school 18
My journey to school 20
Who works in our school? 22
What happens in my school? 24

In the City
Our city 26
Rhythm and movement 28

In the Town
How our town is growing 30
Hidden corners 32
Our town in numbers 34
Local landmarks and abstract art 36

In the Country
Looking at trees 38
Exploring shape through buildings 40
Inspired by landscape artists 42
Working in layers 44

By the Sea
A gallery of seascapes 46
Investigating sand dunes 48
Art on the beach 50
A sea ideas wall 52
A seaside village at war 54

What Happened in My Local Area?
Our market town 56
Homes inspired by Hundertwasser 58
Local memories of the Battle of Britain 60
A royal connection 62

What Can I Do in My Local Area?
Neighbourhood wish tree 64
Hempen homespuns 66
Games from rubbish 68
Recycling your rubbish 70

Introduction

This book explores the idea of neighbours and neighbourhoods. Who are our neighbours? What do they mean to us? Do we know our own local area and can we think of ways to improve it? Examining all the different aspects of neighbourhoods from the geographical to the social, these projects are designed to form part of the wider curriculum.

These projects have been designed by teachers in schools throughout the country in order to look at the widest possible spread of neighbourhoods, from inner city to the most rural. The objective is to give children a way to anchor their learning in a display, which should reflect all the stages of the project, from discussion to final artwork.

Although each project has been devised with a particular age group in mind, special care has been given to show ways of making the ideas appeal to either a younger or older audience. Different children of the same age have different capacities and there are suggestions for stretching the more inquiring and mature children as well as reinforcing learning for the less confident. In the same way, teachers will know the capacities of their own class and it is advised that all activities and materials should be assessed for potential hazards. Children should always be supervised extremely carefully when trying any new technique or when working with certain tools.

Chapter 1 Where Do I Live?

This chapter looks at the global perspective of neighbourhoods. Where do I live in the world? It investigates neighbouring countries and locates the local area firmly through social networks and through map work. It also explores a child's own environment. What is their ideal room?

Chapter 2 What is My School Like?

How do children travel to school? Who works in their school? What happens there and what is it like? Aimed particularly at younger children, there are suggestions for work in numeracy, ICT and literacy, as well as music, art and PSHE.

Chapter 3 In the City
Dramatic and imaginative projects can also be simple. A rhythm and movement display explores what happens when we exercise and fabric reflecting a cityscape can be made with basic stencils.

Chapter 4 In the Town
How does a town grow? Examining transport links, as well as shining a light in hidden corners and looking at local landmarks through the eyes of modern art, help children to discover insights into the place they live.

Chapter 5 In the Country
These projects help children to look before they draw. Investigating the natural world and sharing insights of other well-known artists, children explore techniques such as clay, collage and 3D work.

Chapter 6 By the Sea
Children investigate how to draw the sea, as well as learn about its historical significance in World War 2. They make a scientific survey of the beach, and discover its potential for an Andy-Goldsworthy-inspired installation.

Chapter 7 What Happened in My Local Area?
Here, the children explore what their local area is famous for, through the colourful work of Hundertwasser and also through Tudor portraits and games, as well as tapping into local memories.

Chapter 8 What Can I Do in My Local Area?
Finally, the children investigate what they can do to improve their local area. A project inspired by Yoko Ono's 'Wish Tree' gets children thinking about their community, whilst projects on weaving and home-made toys and games and an investigation into recycling facilities in the local area increase awareness of materials and what we can do with them when they are no longer needed.

Thanks to technology, we are in touch with more people all around the globe. We have more neighbours than ever. This book offers a range of engaging learning activities that allow children to explore their neighbourhood on a geographical and social level. We hope you enjoy the projects as much as we have.

Julie Ashfield, Rebecca Bruce, Sarah Deas,
Nigel Meager, Peter Newbury,
Noel Springett-McHugh,
Stephen Springett-McHugh and Claire van Rhyn

Where Do I Live?

Global neighbours

Today, we are in touch with more people all around the globe. We have more neighbours than ever. Talk about the differences and similarities between cultures, encouraging children to share their heritage and develop confidence in their unique contribution to the world. The giant maps and globe from this project help children to understand the multicultural nature of their world.

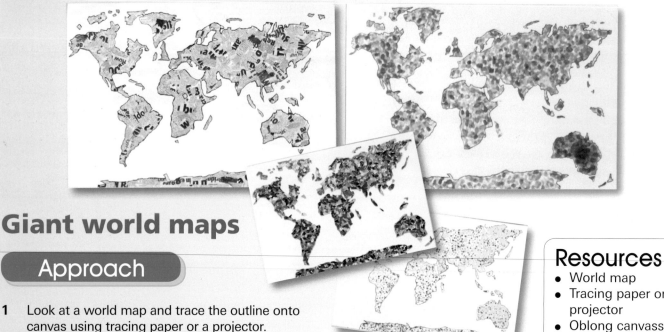

Giant world maps

Approach

1   Look at a world map and trace the outline onto canvas using tracing paper or a projector.

2   Use different techniques to design the map: paint them with finger prints; make a collage with similar coloured paper or newsprint; print with string or bubble wrap.

3   Glaze with watered down PVA glue for a shiny finish.

Resources
- World map
- Tracing paper or projector
- Oblong canvasses
- Scrap paper in different colours
- Paints and palettes
- Bubble wrap
- String
- PVA glue, water

People from around the globe

Approach

1   Discuss cultures from around the world, looking at images of cultural artefacts, clothes, etc.

2   Help children to prepare simple templates for bodies and clothes, asking them to keep in mind a specific culture, maybe one they are familiar with.

3   Use the templates to cut felt into simple body shapes and cut clothes from scrap fabrics.

4   Cut a circle from the fabric and draw a face in felt-tip. Also cut small oblongs where children can draw their cultural artefacts, e.g. a handmade tool or carving.

5   Assemble characters by gluing clothing, the face and cultural artefact onto a body shape. Don't use too much glue, as felt-tip ink can 'bleed'.

Resources
- Felt sheets in different colours
- Patterned scrap fabrics
- Smooth fabric to draw on
- PVA glue
- Scissors
- Black and coloured felt-tips

Stuffed people (see page opposite):
- Child-friendly sewing needles and thread
- Cotton filling or dried lentils

Globe

Approach

1   Blow up a large balloon, e.g. a weather balloon, to the required size and tie a knot to keep it airtight. The knot will form the top of the globe, from which it can be suspended if needed.

2   Cover the balloon with a thin layer of papier mâché, made from white paper strips and papier mâché paste or diluted PVA glue. Once dry, check for strength, adding more papier mâché if needed.

3   Using a map of the world, help children to trace the outlines of the continents onto the globe. Cover the ocean areas with blue tissue paper and stick lentils on the landmasses to give them texture.

4   Sprinkle glitter over water areas to add sparkle. Paint continents in different colours. Cover with diluted PVA to seal and leave to dry. Throughout, make sure the globe remains light enough to suspend.

5   Stick the fabric people onto the globe.

Resources

- Weather balloon
- Strips of white paper
- Papier mâché paste
- PVA glue, water
- World map
- Blue tissue paper
- Glitter
- Dried lentils
- Fabric people (see opposite)

Further ideas

People from around the globe: Older children can make stuffed characters by cutting two body pieces of the same colour felt, sew together and fill.
Globe: Make paper flags on toothpicks to indicate countries. Older children can add more details to the globe, such as mountain ranges built up with papier mâché, names of rivers, cities, etc.

Cross-curricular links

Geography: look at and compare two different countries: physical characteristics, population, natural resources, etc.
Literacy: write about a real or imaginary trip to another country.
PSHE: discuss why we should respect different cultures.

Photographic community portraits

Every day we encounter people in our neighbourhood, but do we really know who they are? With careful planning and supervision, children can interview local individuals about their connection to the area to reveal the knowledge that they have about the neighbourhood. This project collects portraits of the local community.

Create a portrait

Approach

1   Show photographic portraits and discuss what can be discovered about the portrait's subject just by looking at the image. Is there anything in the background which tells us who they are? What are they holding? Can we tell what their emotions are?

2   Encourage children to take portraits of their classmates to get a feel for the process and the results of photography.

3   Discuss what a local neighbourhood is and who makes up the local community.

4   Introduce categories of neighbours. *Do you have friends who live in the neighbourhood? Family? Who might be local business people we know? What about services in the area? Who do we know in our neighbourhood and who might fit into these categories? Who lives next door?*

5   Ask each child to nominate a neighbour and present to their peers the reasons they think this person would be a good subject for a portrait.

6   Select people to photograph. With the help of the school and parents, contact the portrait subjects and request a short interview and photograph. Most local people are likely to know the school and agree.

7   Arrange to either meet at the school, or in the person's daily environment, such as the police station, a shop or library.

8   In small groups, with the support of parents and teachers, conduct interviews with the subjects. *How long have they been living there? What do they like about the neighbourhood?* Record the results.

9   Support children to each take a portrait photograph.

10 Ask each group to select the best photograph to represent each neighbour and write a small biography using the interview information.

11 Print the portrait on normal or photo paper and display with the biography.

Resources
- Examples of good portrait photography
- Digital cameras
- Clipboards and paper
- Pencils
- Computer, colour printer

Portrait album

Approach

1 Cut the walls of two boxes of the same size so that they are 15 cm high. These will form the base of the album.

2 Cover this base in paper and draw lines on the sides to represent the pages of the book. Place the boxes next to each other and stick together with PVA glue.

3 Create a 'cover' for the book by covering corrugated card in old wallpaper. The cover should be slightly wider than the actual book. Staple or glue in place.

4 Cut enough sheets of paper to fit the photographs. These will form the pages of the book. Make sure they match the size of the box base. Sew the pages together.

5 Stick photographs, biographies and names of neighbours onto pages in the book to create an album of local people.

6 Embellish with photo corners and additional photographs.

Resources

- Two large empty boxes
- Large sheets of paper (A1 or A0)
- PVA glue
- Corrugated card
- Roll of old wallpaper
- Spray glue
- Glue stick
- PVA glue
- Computer, colour printer
- Staple gun
- Thick sewing needle
- Embroidery thread

Cross-curricular links

Art and Design: invite a photographer to discuss portrait photography with children. Children like to see real photographic equipment and samples of the photographer's work.

ICT: learn how to collect, download and order digital images on a computer.

PSHE: discuss the idea of privacy and the rights of the individual. Why do we need to take people's privacy seriously?

Mapping community networks

Children are natural explorers. As more information becomes available through the internet and other media, encouraging children to develop structured skills of research and data analysis becomes increasingly important. In these projects, children gather data about the relationships between local people and their neighbourhood and use different ways of visually representing information.

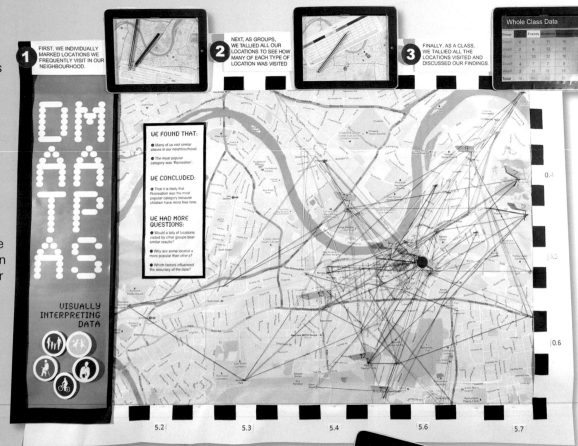

Collect local data

Approach

1 Introduce the idea of data mapping: visual ways of showing information. Show images to illustrate this, e.g. time-lapse photographs showing the movement of traffic in a town or the frequency of airplane flights between countries.

2 Discuss the idea of data gathering: *what is the 'information age' and where does the information come from?* Talk about representing data: *how do we make sense of information and make it accessible to others?* Look at different ways of displaying data, such as info-graphics, interactive data sets and data maps.

3 Gather data on locations which children visit regularly in their neighbourhood. You can create categories such as recreation, family, friends, businesses and services. Give each category a colour and ask children to mark the locations on their individual maps and fill in the locations and categories on a table. Limit the area from which children can choose their locations and exclude their own homes.

4 Divide children into small groups and ask them to tally up the group's total number of locations in each category and discuss their findings.

5 Tally up the whole-class data and discuss the findings: *which categories are most popular and why? How might data gathered by a different group (e.g. working adults instead of school children) differ and why?*

6 Discuss with children how the data could be visually represented so that others could understand the information you have found.

Resources
- Examples of data maps
- Individual data tables (1 per child)
- Maps of the local area (1 per child)
- Group data tables (1 per group)
- Whole-class data table
- Felt-tips

Map the data

Approach

1 On a large-scale map, let each child hammer pins into the locations that they marked on their individual maps.

2 Connect up the pins of the different categories with embroidery thread or ribbon in the category colour.

3 Create a key to show which colour represents which category.

4 If a location is visited by more than one child, develop a way to show this, e.g. a flag with the number of visitors.

5 Ask children to write up their findings from the data and display with the smaller maps and data tables.

Resources

- Mounted large-scale map of the local area (to fit size of display)
- Pins
- Hammer
- Embroidery thread or ribbon in five colours
- Scissors

Further ideas

Practising data handling doesn't need to be abstract. Build physical columns on the ground with younger children and use objects like toys to represent data. Children can physically move 'data' from column to column.

Cross-curricular links

Art and Design: find artists who use data as a theme for their artwork and plan a project around their work.

Geography: when children are familiar with basic map work, introduce online map systems found with popular search engines and plan a route.

PSHE: discuss what a local community is, and what it means to be a neighbour. Talk about ways we are connected and ways that we have become disconnected from our communities.

My town, your town

An interesting way to discuss how your neighbourhood fits into the wider world is to relate it to a neighbourhood in another country. This display looks at a local neighbourhood through the perspective of a modern foreign language. You can choose any country or language as the focus of the project. Why not contact and build a relationship with a school in another country? It will support your pupils in their understanding of how children in other countries live.

Map your neighbourhood

Approach

1   Use a feedback form and group discussions to brainstorm children's ideas about what a local neighbourhood is.

2   Write down key words or phrases from the feedback such as, 'My neighbourhood is urban' or 'My area is called ... ' which can be used to add to the display.

3   Choose a language/country to investigate and work together to translate the words and phrases into your chosen language.

4   Look at a world map to see where your country is in relation to your chosen study country.

5   Using a map of your country, identify your nearest city, town or village, and locate your local neighbourhood.

6   Look at a map of your city, town or village, and locate your local neighbourhood.

7   Arrange map work and drawings together (see page opposite) together with translated words and phrases. Link the buildings shown on the tiles to locations on the map by using wool or embroidery thread. Indicate the location of your school to give context.

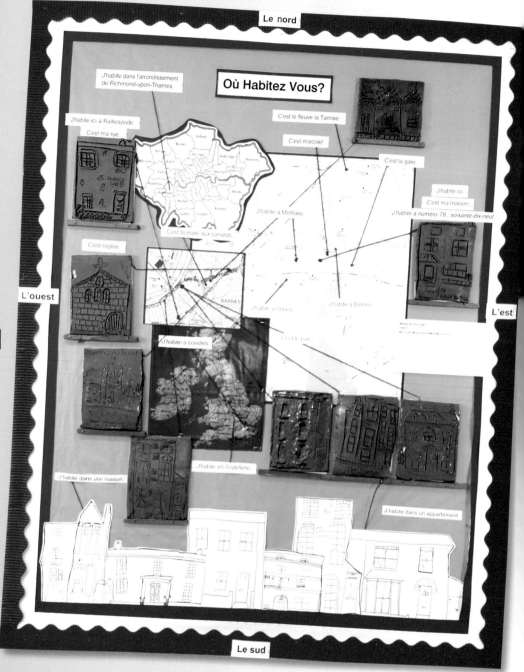

Resources
- Wool or embroidery thread
- Maps
- Tiles (see page opposite)

Clay tiles

Approach

1 In small groups, take children to look at architecture in the local area. If this is not possible, find images of buildings from the local area for children to look at in class. Look at their locations on a map.

2 On loose sheets of paper or in sketchbooks, draw pictures of landmarks or listed buildings from your area in pencil.

3 Draw over the pencil drawings in pen to make the lines more visible. Transfer the drawings to tracing paper for use on the tiles, but keep original drawings to include in the display.

4 Roll clay into 1 cm thick sheets and cut tiles to fit the size of the drawings.

5 Place tracing paper on the tiles and draw over the lines with a blunt pencil to transfer the drawing to the clay.

6 Lift the tracing paper and work deeper into the clay to make the lines more visible with a clay tool.

7 To identify the buildings, write their name or location in the clay. Dry, glaze and fire the clay tiles as resources allow.

Resources
- Pencils
- Thin black felt-tips
- Sketchbooks or loose sheets of paper
- Tracing paper
- Red earthenware clay
- Clay tool
- Rolling pin

Further ideas

If your school has a link with a school in another country, set up a letter exchange. Create a display showing the communication between the children, using images such as stamps, postcards and envelopes to embellish the display.

Cross-curricular links

Art and Design: look at the architectural design of buildings in your local area. Discuss the design differences for each time period represented. Are there any listed buildings and what does it mean to protect your architectural heritage?

Geography: what are the effects of the man-made environment? What do we need to think about when we build new buildings and how could a new development affect your area?

Language Studies: practise basic words and phrases for everyday things around your neighbourhood in a modern foreign language.

My ideal space

In this project, children can imagine their perfect bedroom and begin to think about the design of everyday environments. It is an opportunity for them to express their own style and consider the furniture and objects in people's homes. It also provides practise in planning and implementing a simple project.

Designing a bedroom

Approach

1   Start by looking at images of themed bedrooms and talk about the type of furniture and objects in a bedroom. Show children images of different objects and furniture such as mirrors, curtains, rugs, shelving, clocks, windows, lamps, plants, beds, chairs, etc.

2   Use a mind map to develop ideas about a theme for an ideal bedroom. To help them develop their ideas, ask children to make a presentation to the class of their ideal bedroom, explaining why they made their choices.

3   Go through the scrap materials, asking children to suggest different ways of using them. Using drawings and writing, plan four furniture items from available materials for their ideal room.

4   Choose wallpaper to suit the theme. Discuss how to measure and fit the wallpaper without using a ruler. Cut the wallpaper for the back and side walls and glue into the box. Measure and cut the carpet/floor paper in the same way. Fit and glue into the box.

5   Create four furniture items from available materials according to the room theme, e.g. tables made from thread spools with a disc of cardboard; lamps made from string and cupcake cases; mirrors made from foil; chairs made from egg cartons, etc.

6   Place furniture in the room by tacking or sticking in place. Make holes in the shoebox to stabilise furniture, if necessary.

7   Add finishing touches by creating rugs, mirrors, portraits and other objects.

8   Ask the children to evaluate the four furniture items they have made. *Were they the correct size for the room? How well did they manage to fit their wallpaper, carpets, etc.?*

9   When the rooms are finished, cut star-shaped frames from corrugated card to fit around the outside of the boxes.

10 Spread PVA glue on the frames and sprinkle with glitter. Attach to a display wall. Create additional smaller star shapes to suspend between the room boxes.

Resources

- Images of rooms and furniture
- Scrap paper (wrapping paper, wallpaper, etc.)
- Shoeboxes
- Coloured paper
- PVA glue and glue sticks
- Thin card
- Scrap fabrics
- Empty match/raisin boxes
- String
- Corks
- Straws
- Toothpicks
- Bottle tops
- Foil
- Mini cupcake cases
- Empty thread spools
- Empty egg cartons
- Scissors
- Corrugated card
- Masking tape
- Blue tack
- Glitter

Cross-curricular links

Design and Technology: talk about the idea of interior design and its place in our lives. Who designs all the things we have in our houses? Are the objects we have in our homes used for their function or their form (the way they look), or both? How are these items made: by hand or mass produced?

PSHE: discuss with children what humans need to survive and how these needs are met. Does everyone have all their needs met? What are the differences between needs and wants?

Science: research sustainable housing. Look at the reasons why we are making our houses more sustainable. What changes are happening to the way we build and renovate homes? Which materials do we no longer use and why?

Sounds around our school

The sounds we hear in our school are part of the environment in which we learn. On a walk around the school both inside and outside, ask children to listen to the many different sounds they can hear. Encourage listening and speaking by discussing these sounds. Explain that sound words are called onomatopoeias, for example, the scrape of chair legs across the floor.

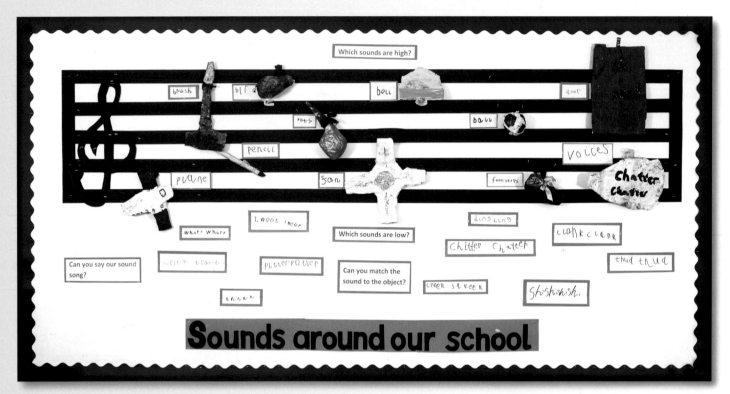

Write music

Approach

van "vvvrm"

1. Take the children on a walk around their school environment.

2. Children record their sounds pictorially on a musical stave in order to compose a piece of music that they can perform aloud. This composition will describe their school (e.g. in a city school they may hear aeroplanes, whereas in the countryside they may hear animals nearby).

3. Write a list of all the sounds that can be heard. Encourage children to use their phonic knowledge to spell out these sounds. They can write their own labels for the sounds.

4. Ask children to notice which sounds are high and which are low.

5. Use a musical stave to chart/record the sounds pictorially.

6. Ask children to 'say' their composition. How do they think it sounds? Reflect on the composition and encourage them to consider if it would make a difference if the sounds were placed in a different order.

7. Once they have a composition they are pleased with, they can perform it aloud.

Resources
- Blank musical stave
- Writing and drawing materials

Sound display

Approach

1   Create a musical stave on a display board.

2   Create three-dimensional newspaper models of whatever has made the sounds, using masking tape to help secure and join the paper where necessary.

3   Use papier mâché paste and more newspaper to secure the models and leave to dry.

4   Paint these, and use felt-tips to add final details when the paint has dried.

5   Using the children's design, plot the objects along the stave, encouraging them to think about whether each one is a high, middle or low sound and secure the objects accordingly using ribbons.

6   Promote the use of the interactive display using questions and prompts: can they perform their work 'reading' the music from the display?

Resources

- Newspapers
- Masking tape
- Papier mâché paste
- Paint and brushes
- Felt-tips
- Ribbons

Further ideas

Explain to younger children that music and notes can be read like a book – each mark has a meaning. Encourage them to practise phonics, segmenting and blending. They could count the sound models in place order: first, second, third, etc.

Practise reading music with older children. Invite them to write a description of what they can hear in the street, using onomatopoeias, and using phonic knowledge to spell 'sound' words. Ask them to count the beats in a bar.

Cross-curricular links

Geography: how do sounds we hear vary according to our environment? Would we hear cars/sirens/aeroplanes in the countryside?

ICT: use an ICT software program to compose music.

Literacy: practise speaking, listening and writing lists.

Music: compose, edit, review and perform a simple piece inspired by a rainy day.

Shapes in our school

During a walk through the school, encourage young children to look for shapes they can recognise in their school building and in the objects they use every day. Let them photograph shapes they recognise. Ask children why certain objects are particular shapes. It is worth pointing out that some 2D shapes they notice may be part of a 3D object; e.g. a 3D desk has many rectangular faces. It is the flat 2D shapes they are looking for in this project.

Shape display

Approach

1   Print the children's photographs and lay them out for sorting.

2   Use labels or large pictures to represent the shapes your class have looked for. Ask children to match their photographs to the label. They should stick these on with glue.

3   Mount these onto a backed display board.

4   Make the display interactive by sticking on additional photos with hook and loop fasteners, with a written invitation to place them correctly (it may be best to laminate these as they will wear out as the children reposition them).

5   Leave extra hook and loop fasteners attached to the board for repositioning.

Resources
- Digital camera
- Printer
- Hook and loop fasteners
- Laminate
- Labels or large pictures
- Glue

Shape books

Approach

1   Make some empty paper books with a front cover.

2   Children can stick their shape photos into the books. Choose how detailed the books should be. Children could group their photos into particular shapes.

3   Children can read or describe their books to a younger/older child or their class peers to foster community spirit within the school.

4   Older children can make their own shape books including information about the properties of shapes.

Resources
- Scrap paper
- Stapler (adult use only)
- Children's photos of shapes
- Drawing and colouring materials
- Glue

Shape mobile

Approach

1   Join two pieces of wood in an 'x' shape. Use blue tack to hold them and bind with string.

2   Attach a loop of ribbon in the middle for hanging up in front of the display.

3   Tie a length of ribbon on each 'arm' of the mobile, one for each shape: circle, square, rectangle, triangle.

4   At the top of each piece of ribbon attach a clear picture/label for the shape children need to sort. They can now fix matching photos of shapes around the school, e.g. the circle ribbon will have up to ten photos hanging down of circles they saw around the school.

5   Suspend the mobile in front of the display.

Resources
- Two thin pieces of wood
- String
- Blue tack
- Ribbon cut to different lengths
- Children's photos of shapes

Cross-curricular links

Geography: look at shapes in both natural and made environments. Is there a correlation between them?

Literacy: Understand and learn about the features of books: including the front and back cover, title, author, imprint page, contents, chapters, page numbers, glossary (for information/non-fiction books) and index.

Maths: focus on the properties of 2D shapes, using correct mathematical vocabulary.

My journey to school

On the way to school, children will recognise their local neighbourhood. They may notice the same people going to work, the same cars, the same cats or pass the same landmarks every day. For this project, encourage children to use their observational skills to create a 3D street view. They can include familiar landmarks and use these as starting points for discussion.

3D display

Approach

1   Using children's ideas, create a 3D backdrop of the street where their school is. This may include a road, trees, lamp posts, signs, etc. which children could themselves draw, paint or create with a collage.

2   Begin by holding a class discussion about what children see on their local street. Discuss what landmarks they see every day.

3   Children are to work in pairs to design and draw a familiar landmark on their school's street such as a house, the school, playground, café, park or tube station. They can then think about what they can use to create their landmark, e.g. cardboard, a stiff plastic sheet, boxes, pots, etc. and how they can join these together.

4 When children have built their landmark, they paint it and add further, finer details in pen once the paint is dry.

5 Back the display board with blue paper for sky and grey paper for the road.

6 Assemble the landmarks and glue them together on the 3D display to create the street.

7 Final touches could include numbering houses. You could also add buses, cars, etc.

Resources

- Scrap materials, e.g. boxes, etc.
- Paints and brushes
- Pens, felt-tips and crayons
- Scissors
- PVA glue

Further ideas

Younger children may find it helpful to go for a walk and take photos as part of the lesson.

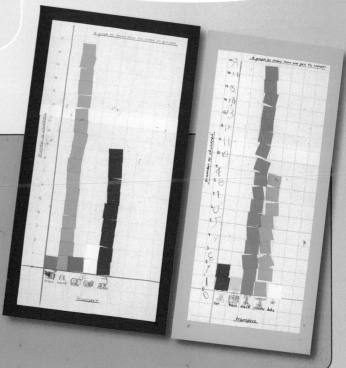

Cross-curricular links

Design and Technology: explore fixing and joining materials.

Geography: make a map of the journey to school, including local landmarks; natural and man-made.

Maths: examine the properties of 3D shapes. Make bar graphs to show the different ways children travel to school, e.g. on foot, by car, etc.

PSHE: discuss things that can scare/frighten children on their way to school.

Who works in our school?

This project gives children an insight into what happens in school outside of their classroom and highlights the importance of teamwork and sharing roles and responsibilities. Support small groups of children as they interview adults employed in different capacities at school, for example: a teacher, teaching assistant, learning support assistant, chef, lunchtime supervisor, caretaker, office staff, lollypop person, etc. Discuss with children beforehand what questions they will ask; encourage them to find out how each adult helps to support the running of the school and how this impacts on the children's own learning. *How many people work at the school?*

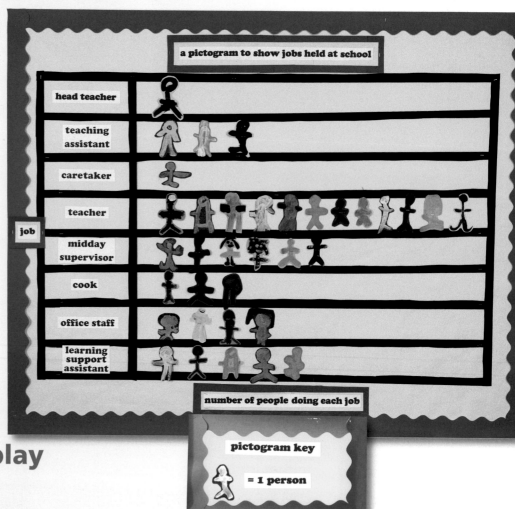

Pictogram display

Approach

1 Children should make notes or record the answers to their interview questions.

2 Once they have information from their interviews, they should use it to create a frequency or tally chart. They should list all the people they have interviewed and the jobs they do.

Resources
- Clipboards and paper
- Paints and brushes
- Scissors
- PVA glue
- Computer
- Printer
- Pencils

3 Create a large-scale pictogram display.

4 Write the jobs down the side of the pictogram. Explain that the chart is going to show how many people do particular jobs at school. In groups, children can create small pictorial 'people'.

5 Ask children to input data onto the pictogram, using the frequency or tally chart.

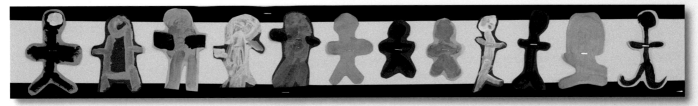

6 Discuss the pictorial key. In larger schools, one picture may need to represent more than one person on the pictogram.

7 Ask children to devise their own questions for interpreting data from the pictogram, e.g. *How many office staff are there in the school?*

8 Ask each child to paint their own portrait of a chosen person. Ensure enough portraits are made to represent everyone interviewed. To provide an interactive element, ask children to write or type information they have discovered from their interviews as labels and add them to the portraits. Display the portraits with the pictogram.

Further ideas

Encourage older children to ask questions such as *How do members of staff get to school? How far do they travel?* They could carry out a survey and use the information to make a chart.

Cross-curricular links

Geography: draw a map of your school and where everyone works, using a key.

ICT: use computer software to make different types of graphs. Are all graphs/charts appropriate for all information, or do some work better than others?

Literacy: ask children to write an account of a time when they worked as a team.

PSHE: discuss the importance of team work. What jobs are best done as a team?

What happens in my school?

This project is designed to develop children's understanding of the physical space of their school by planning and designing their own school out of 'junk' materials. Begin by discussing prominent features of the school building: *does it have a flat or pointed roof? How could children show this using the materials they have?* Ask them to make a list of all the rooms in use in their school. *As they move around during the day, what do they notice happening in these rooms? Who uses them? Are they used for more than one activity or purpose?* Encourage children to think about appropriate ways of making separate rooms, and how they could join the parts of the building together.

Once the shell of their school building is complete, they can design furniture using a range of materials depending on age and ability (wood, clay, or plasticine). Finally, they can use the school for imaginative play, role playing familiar, new or difficult scenarios, or presenting puppet performances.

3D school

Approach

1   Choose boxes and junk modelling material in appropriate size and shape.

2   Cut the boxes as necessary and fix any boxes together to make second or third floors.

3   Cut out shapes for the windows (an adult should do this).

Resources

- Selected 'junk' materials including cardboard boxes and clear plastic
- Scissors
- Craft knife (adult use only)
- Masking tape
- Whiteboard marker
- Paint and brushes
- Felt-tips and coloured pens
- Floor covering (lino/carpet)
- PVA glue
- Scraps of plasticine or clay
- Small world materials

4 Use clear plastic for window glass. Cut this to the appropriate size and fix to the inside of the boxes using masking tape.

5 With a whiteboard marker, sketch in lines for window frames.

6 Mix colours and paint the outside and inside of the building. Add extra detail with felt-tips.

7 Cut lino or carpet to the appropriate size and shape to cover the floors. Fix this to the base of the box with PVA glue.

8 Design and create internal details such as pictures on the walls, clocks, etc.

9 Create furniture out of clay or other modelling materials and position as required.

10 Introduce small world scenarios for children to practise using props.

Cross-curricular links

Design and Technology: write an account of how you made the school model, including planning.

History: research the history of your school. How old is it? Were the rooms always where they are now?

Literacy: write a play or story about the school to be 'presented' by small world people.

Maths: discuss how to make more accurate scale models using ratios.

PSHE: using role-play scenarios, puppets or small world people, children can practise how to deal with problems that arise in school.

In the City

Our city

Take some time to discuss with children what it means to live in a city. Look at images of recognisable cityscapes from around the globe, e.g. Paris, New York, London, Tokyo, etc.

Preparing stencils for fabric printing

Approach

1   Take children out into the city to take photos of the landmarks and buildings. Download children's photos and select images which show the landmarks clearly. Resize to similar proportions. Print out the images and cut out the landmarks from the background. If this is not possible, look at images of landmarks and discuss the layout of the city. Encourage children to draw landmarks, then photocopy them so other buildings are similarly sized. Cut buildings out.

2   Choose five landmarks to combine into a design by laying the cut-outs in a cluster arrangement. Overlap them to create a realistic city effect.

3   Each child can also plan an individual design in their sketchbook or on a sheet of paper using smaller versions of the landmark images.

4   Select a design with children and make five separate stencils.

5   Place each of the five cut-out landmark pictures on a separate piece of card and trace, ensuring that the card is at least 5 cm larger than the image on all sides.

6   Cut out the inside of the traced landmark shape leaving a stencil frame.

Resources
- Digital cameras or printouts of city landmarks
- Scissors
- Card

Fabric printing

Approach

1 Choose a contrasting colour for each landmark.

2 Work out how to repeat the pattern across the fabric. Diagonally repeat-printing the whole design gives an organised, staggered appearance, but you could also print horizontally or vertically. With a pencil, discreetly mark where to put the stencils on the fabric.

3 Start by printing the first stencil in the lightest colour. Place the stencil on the fabric and hold in place with masking tape. If the stencil is gaping, stick down with blue tack to ensure no paint goes under the stencil.

4 Sponge paint or ink over the stencil, making sure not to go over the outside edges of the card. Sponge slowly and build up the colour.

5 Carefully remove the wet stencil, preventing it from touching the fabric again.

6 When the paint has dried, continue with the next landmark stencil, building up the design from light to dark colours, each time waiting for the paint to dry before printing the next stencil.

7 Once the entire design cluster has been printed, repeat the process until the fabric is covered in the repeat-design.

Resources

- Large, ironed fabric for printing
- Printing ink or paint
- Printing trays or plastic plates
- Stencils (see opposite page) and pencils
- Sponges
- Masking tape
- Blue tack

Further ideas

Print a cityscape on a canvas. Arrange the landmark prints to mimic the city layout. Draw details of buildings with black pen or print with more than one colour per landmark to build up architectural detail.

Make an imaginative class painting of your city. Show landmarks, activity, vehicles and city dwellers to portray the hustle and bustle of city life.

Cross-curricular links

Art and design: in our digital culture, photography is commonplace. Talk to children about being visually literate and being able to 'read' the information photos offer us.

Geography: discuss the differences between a town, a city and smaller settlements such as villages and hamlets. Look at statistics of how many people live in cities and query why so many people live there.

Rhythm and movement

The frenetic pace of city living is often thought of as negative; however, it can also be seen as a display of energy, rhythm and movement. Physical Education (PE) is frequently neglected in school displays, yet movement is such an integral part of how children interact with the world. Explore the excitement and pace of city living in this fun and informative PE lesson.

A cityscape of PE equipment

Approach

1 Show children images of a city and life in the city. Talk about pace and movement in cities. Use simple exercises to experiment with the different rhythms of a city, e.g. walking fast or slowly in groups or individually, as people might do in rush hour.

2 Set up a cityscape in the school hall or in the playground using PE and gym equipment. Look at a map of your city and try to mimic the layout and landmarks with the equipment. The layout should allow for different routes to be taken through the 'city'. Try to make each route unique by allocating specific movements that need to be used to travel from one landmark to another. Try to keep it simple, yet varied.

3 Work out a direction of travel and 'traffic' rules for the city course.

4 Draw up a simple map of the layout of your 'city' and photocopy for each group. In groups, ask children to plan their travel across the city from one point to another. Offer them a 'menu' of movements, which they can allocate to different routes, e.g. marching, hopping, rolls, etc.

Resources
- Selection of PE and gym equipment
- Images of landmarks and life in a city
- Map of your city

5 You could also allocate character roles to inform the movements, e.g. cyclist, business person, bus driver, tourist, etc.

6 Ask each group to take their turn to navigate the city course and then evaluate their choice of movements on completion.

Movement display

Approach

1 Ask children to write explanations for each of the movements in their chosen route.

2 Scale and print pictures of city landmarks or ask children to paint buildings to fit the display size. Cut out images.

3 Photograph children doing the different movements and scale them so that the children look as if they are interacting with the landmarks, e.g. jumping over, crawling under, etc. Scale, print, and cut out the images.

4 Arrange the layout of the images of the children and landmarks together with the 'movement menu' and children's writing included.

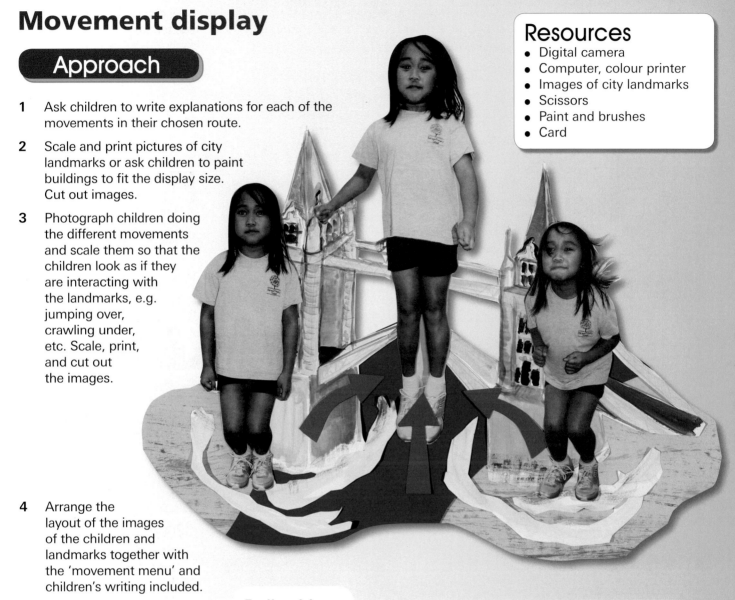

Further ideas

Introduce younger children to simple forces of push and pull.

Let older children experiment with gravity, mass, rotation forces and friction in exercise.

Cross-curricular links

Design and Technology: using shoe boxes as a base, build moving replicas of cityscapes incorporating levers and sliders to make moving people, vehicles and buildings.

Maths: ask children to use timers to measure the time between the different locations and calculate how long it takes to travel different routes.

Science: investigate and discuss how gravity affects movement.

How our town is growing

Mapping transport links is a great starting point for looking at how your town is growing, as this is where most growth takes place. You can even predict how the town may grow in the future. Use the iconic London Underground map to hook children into the learning, together with work from the artist Mondrian to show your town's growth in an exciting and vibrantly abstract style.

Town maps

Approach

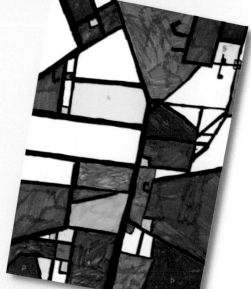

1 Familiarise yourself with images of the London Underground map and the work of Mondrian to inspire and involve children. Share with children and encourage them to identify key features. For example, Mondrian uses block colours, white between bright colour blocks and black lines; an underground map uses diagrammatic coloured lines and black for major junctions.

2 Discuss different areas of the town such as retail, industry, housing, etc. and create a key with a colour representing each area.

Resources
- Maps of the local town
- Mondrian artwork
- Image of the London Underground map
- A4 plain paper
- Pencils
- Black felt-tips
- Coloured felt-tips or another choice of media
- A1 (or larger) white paper or card
- A4 yellow paper
- computer, printer

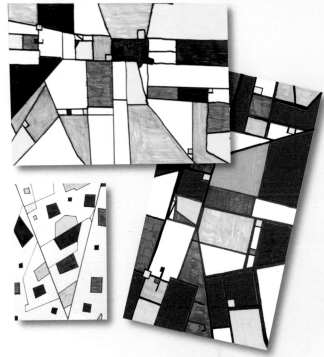

3 Using a map of your local town, model how to draw the main roads on A4 paper. Colour in an area (such as retail) and encourage children to block the different areas on their maps in colour, using their key. Explain that not all of the map should be coloured, as you are just showing representative areas. Remind children of Mondrian's work, where blocks of colour are broken up with areas of white, and display this for children to refer to.

4 Outline all areas and roads in black pen. Once again, link this back to the work of Mondrian.

5 Back children's work and your display board in black to maximise impact. Print out lettering for the heading in yellow.

6 For the A1 display, follow the same instructions on a larger scale with groups of children.

7 Display the large map and small maps together and children can then add printed captions.

Further ideas

Make predictions of how children think the town may grow and create a new map.

- Draw a large rectangle on A1 white card. Ask children to copy their town from the large group map. Refer to previous work, discussing with children how their town might look in five years, ten years, when they are 30 and so on.
- Discuss the communication/transport links. How could the concept of the London Underground map be used on this map? Each coloured line could represent a different communication line, e.g. blue for motorways, green for cycleways, black for A roads, etc.
- Decide on a key and draw shapes representing current areas such as retail, industry, parks, etc.
- Children can now show how they think the town will grow by sticking coloured cut-out shapes along the communication lines and building up new areas of the town.

Cross-curricular links

Citizenship: survey residents about changes to traffic planning.

Dance: using coloured ribbons, create a dance representing transport and movement.

History and Geography: research the development of the town in groups, each with a different time span, each creating a map. Display all the maps together.

Literacy: write a descriptive account of travelling through the town; what you would see, hear, feel and experience. Write a persuasive letter to the town planners against or in support of a major local plan.

Maths: overlay co-ordinates onto your finished maps and create a co-ordinates treasure hunt.

Hidden corners

Children often notice unusual places that don't always turn up on a map. Using photographs and their imagination, ask them to report on areas of their town that they know about but adults don't. This work can be a stimulus for descriptive writing, poetry or even as the scene for a story. Displaying 'their' locations on an aerial map of the town can generate a lot of interest within the wider school audience, who will then identify hidden corners of their own.

Local hide-outs

Approach

1   Collect images from the local town and share them with children to generate a discussion about places where they play (encourage them to bring in photos of their own to add to the image bank).

2   Identify spaces on a local map and ask children to mind map the types of things they do there, e.g. play football, meet friends, chat, play hide and seek, etc.

Resources
- Satellite map image of town centre
- Ruler
- Black marker pen to draw map
- A4 white paper
- Mounting paper
- A2 sheets of buff sugar paper
- Brown corrugated cardboard and green poster roll for trunk and top of tree
- Coloured drawing pins
- String or white wool

3   Research poems about local places, Labraitio Jones's 'Hidden Corners' and 'Somewhere I Don't Go' are useful examples). Discuss any features and uses of language that children could use in their own work.

4   Encourage children to write a poem describing their 'hidden corner'.

5   Using a satellite map, recreate the centre of the town on a sheet of sugar paper.

6   Draw images of a park, or research suitable clip art online and decorate either side of the town map.

7   Display children's work and photographs around the map, using string to pinpoint their locations.

Places to avoid

Approach

1   Ask children if there are any areas of the local town where they wouldn't play with their friends. Explain that avoiding certain areas is one way of keeping themselves safe. Ask them to devise other 'rules' or good advice to keep safe.

2   Review their ideas and add in anything that they may have missed.

3   Create an alleyway scene to depict a place children should avoid.

4   Chalk the outline of a tree on black sugar paper.

5   On red backing paper draw a series of lines radiating out from a central point to create brickwork and perspective.

6   Ask children to write and draw their ideas up on small 'leaflets', or print out notices. Display everything on the walls of the alleyway.

Resources
- Black sugar paper
- Chalk
- Red paper for walls of the alleyway, blue paper for the sky
- Yellow and green paper for lettering and notices

Cross-curricular links

Citizenship: ask children to talk to older family members and neighbours about where they used to play.

ICT: children could use their photos to make a tourist leaflet.

Literacy: children choose hidden sites to create an alternative sightseeing tour for visitors to their town.

PSHE: discuss ways to keep ourselves safe when out and about, reminding children of things they shouldn't do, and people they can trust.

Our town in numbers

Create an interesting maths display to provide insights into your community. Using data handling as the focus, children make a survey of their town, collecting statistical information about its inhabitants, opinions and use of the local environment. This can be based on a class, or broadened to include a year group or even the entire school. Once data has been gathered, use maths lessons to explore percentages, fractions and ratios, graphs and charts to draw out interesting statistics for the display, e.g. *Did you know that 82% of Year Five pupils walk to school?*

Town survey

Approach

1 Design a survey with the children by encouraging them to come up with questions, both obvious (*how do you get to school?*) and more fun (*how many taps are there in your house?*). Agree on a final set of simple questions and type them up.

2 Ask children to fill in the survey for homework. (It is wise to check with colleagues to avoid any sensitive issues, particularly if the survey is intended for the whole school.)

3 Divide children into groups, asking each one to choose a question and tally the information to create a set of data.

4 Use the data for exploring percentages, fractions and ratios. Children can also represent the information as charts and graphs.

5 Create a townscape scene, using clip art or children's art. Cut out and mount artwork on the display board, together with the children's work.

11% of Year 5 live ouside of town

Did you know?

We have 1.7 cars between us

3/5 of Year 5 have 6 taps at home

82% of us walk to school

Our streets have an average 38 houses

Over 3/4 of us use the park

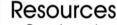

58 % of the Year Group have 3 bedrooms

Resources
- Questions about the local area
- Blue, yellow and green rolls of paper for sun, sky and earth
- A3 coloured paper/ card for the clouds
- Computer, colour printer
- Publisher software
- Coloured paper for lettering, key statistic signs and mounting

Garden design

Approach

1 Ask children to plan and design an imaginary garden. Give children a plot size, a budget and a made-up garden centre catalogue with a list of basic items to 'buy' for their imaginary garden. (Include expensive and cheap versions of each item and give plant sizes, so children can calculate how much space they need.)

2 Ask children to complete a budget sheet. If they want to include items not on the list, agree cost and size with them so they can adjust their budgets.

3 Ask children to work out simple but accurate garden designs on the squared paper.

4 Encourage children to paint large flowers in bright colours; back them on black sugar paper. Mount their garden designs, budget sheets and a copy of the catalogue and add everything to the display.

Resources
- Garden centre 'catalogue'
- Sugar/white paper for the flowers
- Bright, ready-mix paint colours
- Squared paper
- Coloured felt-tips
- Black sugar paper to back the flowers
- Blue paper for lettering and mounting

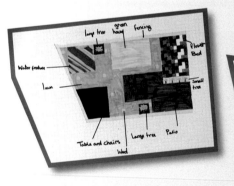

Further ideas

Create a real garden in the school grounds, based on the design of the imaginary garden.

Cross-curricular links

Citizenship: children can support a local charity, planning and carrying out an event to raise money.

History: look at census records to compare data from the past with today. Look at three families and ask children to find three facts the same and three that are different from their own family.

Literacy: use information from their survey to write a persuasive letter, e.g. to the council asking for more play equipment.

Maths: using a collection of teacher prepared diagrams of gardens, get children to calculate the area and perimeter of the garden in each picture.

Local landmarks and abstract art

Every town has desirable local landmarks and some that are less so! This project gets children thinking about their local landmarks, why they are famous and whether their reputation is justified. Starting with a walk around their town, children take photos of buildings, trees and streets which stand out, or are significant in any way and make notes of what they see. In class, create a list of key landmarks, looking at photos and making sketches before encouraging children to manipulate the images into abstract pop art.

Town landmarks

Approach

1   Show the children images of famous landmarks, discussing what a landmark is and where they might exist in your town.

2   Walk around your local town with your class, encouraging children to take photos of landmarks and make notes.

3   Print the photos and ask children to make sketches. Encourage them to talk and listen to each other and discuss what makes these chosen buildings stand out.

4   Outline the sketches with a black pen.

5 Share examples of abstract art from Wassily Kandinsky, Fernand Leger and Georges Braque, discussing how these artists distort the realistic image. Using 2D shapes and either felt-tips or oil pastels, encourage children to represent their landmark in an abstract style.

6 Back children's work on black sugar paper and display on large shapes in different colours.

7 Type out labels for the landmarks on a computer, and print out on blue paper. Print out the heading for the display as large as possible and cut out each letter individually, leaving a 0.5 cm space around the outlines. Display on the board.

Resources
- Sketchbooks/notebooks
- Cameras
- Computer software and printer
- A4 white and blue paper
- 2D shapes/ felt-tips/ oil pastels
- Black sugar paper
- Four sheets of backing paper (different colours)
- Pencils and thin black pens

Further ideas

Use the drawings to create a fun game that gets children to tap into their knowledge of local landmarks.
- Ask children to write questions on the computer about local landmarks depicted in their display.
- Print out the questions, and place them in an open folder with a large question mark on it. Attach to a display board.
- Add numbers 1–6 to the board and put a photograph, line drawing or coloured picture of a local landmark underneath each number.
- Children can test one another on their local knowledge and win points for correct answers. You can change pictures and questions every week.

Cross-curricular links

Art: children can use abstract images to describe feeling either proud or angry.

Citizenship: arrange a visit from someone from the council to talk to children about any issues the town is facing and any new developments planned for the town's future.

History: research a fact file about the important buildings in the town. When and why were they built?

Literacy: describe an imaginary meeting between the builder of the oldest landmark and the newest landmark.

In the Country

Looking at trees

In a rural setting, investigating trees is an ideal way to develop a range of children's art skills, such as observational drawing and exploring lines, as well as using a variety of graphic media. In this chapter, each project builds in some way on the next, although they can be used individually. It is very important to explain to children that the finished product is not the only focus. The actual journey of making is a learning process in itself. Therefore this project also develops wider skills, including research, using a camera, independent and collaborative working, and vocabulary and communication.

Collaborative tree paintings

Approach

1. Discuss different kinds of lines. Ask children to look around and suggest different lines to draw, such as: straight, curly, zigzag and diagonal. Collect their ideas on paper.

2. Use their vocabulary to create a word cloud, using one of the online sites, such as 'Wordle'.

3. Prepare children for working outside the classroom and check that everyone knows how to use the school cameras. Explain that they are looking for examples of different types of lines and they won't be photographing landscapes or whole trees. Every child should take at least two photographs.

4. Divide the class into small groups and with adults go out into the school grounds or local area. Make sure that children have easy access to paper, drawing boards, marker pens and a camera. Then, by observing trees, each child should collect lines by drawing and taking photos.

5. Back in the classroom, pupils download their photos to create a slide show, to act as a stimulus for discussion about the quality of the photos. *Which are the most successful shots? How could some photos be improved?*

6. Split children into pairs provide several large A1 sheets of paper for them to make large whole-tree drawings, based on their outside work.

7 Next, each group should develop a large-scale collaborative tree picture. To create this, roll backing paper along the full length of the classroom tables, or children could work on the floor. Encourage them to be imaginative and listen to the ideas of others.

8 Discuss with children what should be included, and how it should be put together. Remember that the display should tell the story of how the work was created from initial starting points to final outcomes. Cut out the large group tree drawings as the base of the display, then add photographs, initial sketches and captions explaining anything which children have noted.

Resources
- Computer
- Cameras
- Graphic media: soft pencils, marker pens, charcoal, graphite sticks and black wax crayons
- Drawing boards
- A1 paper
- Good quality A3 paper
- Long rolls of backing paper

Cross-curricular links

Geography: research the impact of cutting down trees. What do we use wood for? Where are the oldest trees in the village?

History: look at historical maps to see how your district has changed. How were local people living 500 years ago?

Literacy: make a storyboard or write an account of the process of making the display.

Science: research how a tree grows.

Exploring shape through buildings

In many villages, there are buildings that are significant to the whole community. Investigating a church, for example, provides an ideal opportunity for children to explore visual elements including: lines, shapes, patterns and textures. Shape is the focus for this project and specific skill development includes making sketchbooks, taking photographs, using mind maps to encourage more in-depth thinking about the location, as well as finished artwork.

Exploring shapes in local buildings

Approach

1   This project documents the process of discovery and exploration. Prepare for a visit to the village church by making mini folded-paper sketchbooks. Explain to children that their sketchbooks are for collecting information and ideas, and to record what they hear and also how they feel.

2   Before going out, talk about looking for and collecting shapes. *What shapes do children know?* Mathematical shapes will be readily recalled: squares, rectangles, triangles, circles, semi-circles and ovals. Other shapes are recognised by their outline, e.g. gates, bushes, rooftops. Explain to children that the visit is for research. They are collecting ideas and information to use for making pictures after the visit.

3   At the church, children work in groups using mini folded-paper sketchbooks, marker pens and cameras to collect drawings and photographs of outline shapes, for example, shapes of windows, doorways, gates, archways and bushes.

4 Back in the classroom, lay out the children's sketchbooks for the class to look at and download their photographs to create a slide show.

5 Set up groups to develop collaborative A1 mind maps about the visit to the village church, using ideas from the children's sketchbooks. Display the mind maps together with the books and photographs to inspire children when they are working on the next step.

6 Each child should now create his or her own A3 imaginative church drawing.

Resources
- Cameras
- Extra adults for supervision
- Computer, printer
- A1 and A3 paper
- Graphic media: marker pens, pencils, oil pastels, drawing inks

Cross-curricular links

Art and Design: compare the way two different artists portray buildings, e.g. Edward Hopper and John Piper.

History: research either the oldest or the biggest building in your area. What does it tell you about how people lived in the past?

Literacy: imagine what it would be like to work on a big building project such as a castle or cathedral in the Middle Ages. Write a short story about it from the perspective of the builder.

Maths: examine and name some of the regular shapes children have discovered. What solid objects are associated with them?

Science: examine the archways in a church. Why are they so important?

Inspired by landscape artists

Looking at the work of established artists helps children to see the world around them in a different way. It helps them to develop a greater understanding of their own work whilst broadening their knowledge of different art forms. This project looks in detail at two artists: John Piper and David Nash. Piper lived in Epsom, Surrey and, as a child, he often explored the area on his bike, drawing and painting pictures of old churches and monuments on the way. Nash is a British sculptor, based in Wales, who has worked worldwide with wood, trees and the natural environment.

Comparing artists

Approach

1 Encourage children to explore clay, ink and pastel, looking at two established artists. Try to choose at least one local artist. The display in the photo features a local artist, David Nash, and John Piper whose work includes colourful paintings of churches as well as stained glass.

2 Ask children to make a word cloud about the chosen local artist, e.g. David Nash.

3 Arrange a visit to a local gallery. The children in this photograph visited an exhibition by David Nash.

4 Allow children to see first-hand the artist's work and examine how it was crafted, e.g. look closely at a David Nash sculpture and see how he has used a chainsaw to create linear patterns. Ask them to draw what they see.

5 Back in the classroom, using what they have learned from their gallery visit, together with photographs and the drawings they have made, ask children to create their own artist-inspired design. The children in the photographs chose to make tree designs, inspired by David Nash's sculptures.

6 Explain to children that they are now going to turn their designs into clay tiles. Use a tile cutter to prepare slabs of clay for each child. An additional half slab of clay per child is needed to create tree designs. Encourage children to use clay tools to cut the clay into strips and lay them on top of the base slab.

7 When children are happy with their designs, glue each strip down individually with clay glue or slip. Slip is made by mashing small pieces of clay in a pot with a small amount of water until it is the consistency of double cream. Score the back of each part of the design with a pointed clay tool and paint on a generous amount of slip. Score the base tile in the same way and paint with slip. Press each piece onto the tile base until the design is complete. Additional texture and patterns can be added with clay tools.

8 Show children images of the other chosen artist's work, e.g. John Piper. Ask them to make a word cloud. *What do they notice about this artist's work?*

9 Using their sketchbook ideas from the shapes in churches project on page 40, children can make their own pictures inspired by their second chosen artist on A3 paper, using marker pens, coloured inks or oil pastels.

10 Include children's clay tiles and A3 pictures, together with information about work by the two artists in the display. Include photos of the children working and captions documenting how children made their tiles and artwork.

Resources

- Images of the chosen artists' work
- Earthenware clay
- Clay tools
- Slip
- Tile cutter
- Paper
- Sketchbooks (see page 40)
- Drawing boards
- Oil pastels
- Drawing inks and brushes

Cross-curricular links

Art: research the work of another local artist.

History: investigate stained-glass windows from medieval times to the present day.

Science: research how different substances react when heated or cooled, when water is added or when they are dried out.

Working in layers

In this project, children learn to make decisions about how they will respond to their village and its environment, and apply perspective. It shows how to represent a locality in 3D by creating layers of collage that stand up like scenery on a stage. Looking at the work of fellow pupils and discussing it helps children learn from their peers. This is a valuable transferable skill in itself, but it also supports pupils as they take their creativity to another level.

Landscape collage

Approach

1   Discuss perspective before children begin. Look out of the classroom window and ask children what they see furthest away in the distance – it may be the skyline, trees and rooftops. *What can be seen in the middle ground? And finally, what is in the foreground?*

2 Now talk with children about the characteristics of their locality. *Is it hilly or flat, wooded, agricultural, urban, or a mixture?* Look at local maps and photos, including children's photos from the previous projects. *What are the most significant landmarks? How can they convey this location to others?*

3 Discuss the technique of mixed media collages with children, which involves adding colour and drawing onto a collage of their photocopied photos.

4 Demonstrate tearing the photocopied photos apart by hand to create a rough edge – no scissors! Then arrange the pieces onto a strip of paper, leaving intentional gaps to fill in with drawing.

5 Lay out all the photocopies of resource materials collected and let children sort it into categories, e.g. general landscape, the church and churchyard, the river and the bridge.

6 Working in groups, children should choose a collection of photocopies to work with. Each group should split into three sub-groups to create a foreground, a middle ground or a background.

7 Provide the opportunity for groups to decide on the scale, from A4 up to A1. Working on a large scale can be very liberating, but remember that different children prefer to work at different scales.

8 Depending on the chosen size, prepare three strips of cartridge paper or thin card, graduating in height. The narrowest strip will be for the foreground team to work on.

9 Ask children to tear their chosen photocopies and put the pieces in position on the card, as you previously demonstrated.

Resources

- Photocopies of children's black and white / colour photos of landmarks or features in their local area
- Local maps
- Graphic media: coloured drawing inks, pens, oil pastels, brushes
- PVA glue
- Backing paper and A4, A3 or A1 cartridge paper
- Card
- Masking tape

10 Next, they should glue the pieces down, and begin drawing onto the collage and adding colour, either pastel or coloured ink. These are experimental collage drawings, so explain to children that they shouldn't worry about making precise pictures. It is the overall effect which is important.

11 When completed, children should secure the strips of paper in place with masking tape on one side only, onto a card base. They should be able to stand upright or lie flat. Tape the middle ground layer in front of the distance layer, leaving a gap, before placing the foreground.

Cross-curricular links

Design and Technology: build other 3D environments, e.g. a scene from a favourite book or film.

Literacy: imagine walking through one of the collage environments you have created. Write a story about returning to your area way into the future. What would you find?

A gallery of seascapes

The sea is a powerful and beautiful influence for all those who live nearby. This project explores how to give the impression of the movement of water by experimenting with different drawing media, and then creating sea pictures for a class gallery.

Create a seascape

Approach

1   Before getting started, show video extracts of the sea and read literature that describes the sea. Get the children thinking about the different moods the sea might have, from flat calm through to choppy, through to the most violent storm. Encourage them to make wave movements with their arms, hands and fingers.

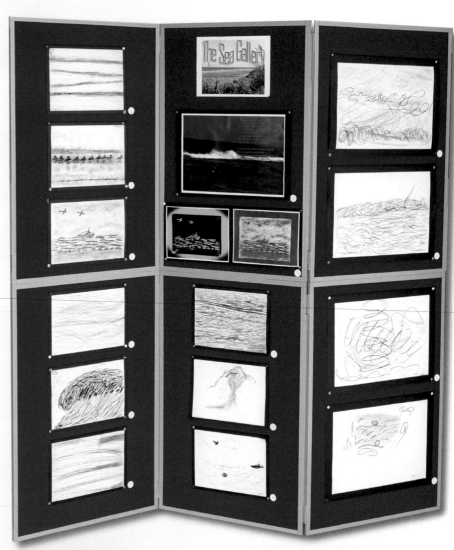

2   Give children a selection of drawing media to explore, e.g. charcoal, soft pencils, and black handwriting pens. Without actually drawing the sea, ask them to experiment with the media to create the different lines and marks which might show how the sea moves or how the surface of the sea looks. As inspiration, you could show them adult artists' drawings and paintings of the sea. However, leave children as free as possible to explore their own techniques in ways which work for them.

3   Have an informal exhibition of the work so far and talk about the ideas and different ways of working children have discovered. Encourage sharing approaches and the idea that they can learn a lot from each other.

4   Children can now create their first sea drawing. They may like to work collaboratively on larger drawings.

5   Using a limited colour palette, show children how to dilute the inks. Practise using brushes and ink on scrap paper first.

6   Children can scan their drawings and work on them digitally. Explain that changes in mood and atmosphere can be achieved by altering colours and applying different filter effects.

7   After writing poetry, invite children to come up with words or phrases to be added to their drawings.

8   Mount a formal exhibition of the visual imagery on screens and create a printed catalogue. Number each image and include an entry for every work, with the name of the artist, the media used, the size, the title and a brief explanation or description.

Resources

- Video extracts of the sea
- Descriptive writing about the sea
- Graphic media: hand writing pens, soft drawing pencils, charcoal
- Drawing boards
- A3 and A2 paper
- Coloured ink and ink containers
- Thin and thick soft brushes
- Scrap paper
- Scanner
- Printer
- Adult art showing different ways of rendering the sea

The big wave getting ready to sweep away the world.

The ship is feeling lonely in the dark

Cross-curricular links

Art and Design: create a huge collaborative drawing of the sea.

Literacy: write poems about the sea, listen to and read extracts of adult writing about the sea.

Science: explore the sea: research currents, tides, waves and how they are created, sea creatures and plants, and list seas around the world.

Investigating sand dunes

The beach can be an excellent environment for a range of learning activities. This project and the one that follows on page 50 combine the fields of science and art by encouraging children to explore the beach and surrounding dunes. This first project takes the form of a science investigation.

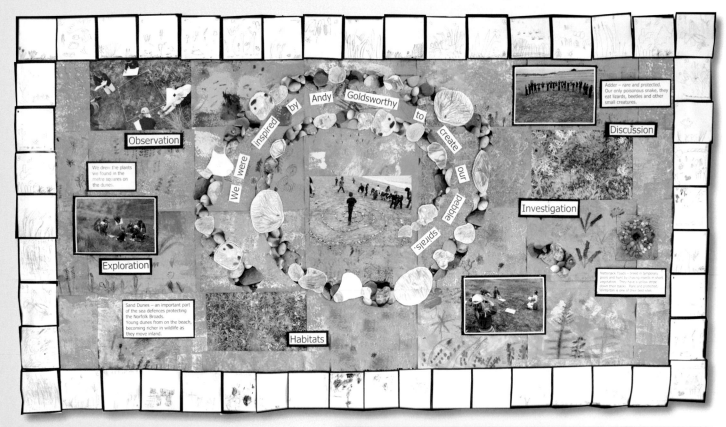

We were inspired by Andy Goldsworthy to create our pebble spirals.

Observation

We drew the plants we found in the metre squares on the dunes.

Exploration

Sand Dunes – an important part of the sea defences protecting the Norfolk Broads. Young dunes from on the beach, becoming richer in wildlife as they move inland.

Habitats

Adder – rare and protected. Our only poisonous snake, they eat lizards, beetles and other small creatures.

Discussion

Investigation

Natterjack Toad – breed in temporary pools and hunt by chasing insects in short vegetation. They have a yellow stripe down their backs. Rare and protected. Winterton is one of their best sites.

Close-up of a dune

Approach

1   Before children visit the dunes with adult supervision, find a suitable place for the class to work and mark out six areas (each approximately 1 m square) for their investigations. Use string and wooden pegs and ensure there is enough room for each group to have its own space to explore.

2   When children arrive, ask them to talk about everything they can see in the marked-out area. Ask the children to point out the different kinds of leaves and look at some of the smaller plants with magnifying glasses. See what else they discover in their area.

3   Divide the A3 paper into six sections. Give the children A3 drawing boards (made out of thin plywood) and have them tape their paper to these boards with masking tape. Get each group to record what they find on one part of the paper. After ten minutes or so, have the groups swap areas.

4   Have everyone take at least one photograph. Ensure the adults take good photographs of each marked area. Enlarge the photos later for the display.

5   Back in the classroom, ask children to recreate the myriad textures they found by printing with a whole selection of textured surfaces. Use them as a backdrop for the display. Add children's drawings and photographs. See page 50 for more information about the Andy-Goldsworthy-inspired spiral.

Resources
- Parent helpers
- String
- Wooden pegs
- Magnifying glasses
- A3 drawing boards
- A3 paper divided into six sections
- Masking tape
- Pens and soft drawing pencils
- Cameras
- Enlarged photographs
- Paints and textured surfaces to make prints

Habitats

Cross-curricular links

ICT: photography is an integral part of this project. Children can learn about keeping files, naming images and how to use images as part of a science investigation.

Literacy: write reports about their investigation explaining how they went about their work and what they discovered.

Science: investigate how the dunes were made and describe the plants and animals that live there.

Art on the beach

These projects are all about the beach and involve a visit to the sand dunes which can also be integrated into a science investigation (see page 48). Children can make collections of beach material to create their own beach in the classroom. The second, more advanced project, requires children to make their own version of an Andy Goldsworthy installation.

Nature in art

Approach

1. Organise a trip to the beach and have each child bring a small carrier bag. With adult supervision, get children to explore the beach from the dunes right up to the sea shore. Have everyone take photographs. Ensure children don't pick up anything inappropriate or dangerous.

2. Using the materials found at the beach, have children collaborate to make their own beach, deciding where the various found materials could be placed. After making a large collaborative beach with adult support, you could ask children to make their own beaches independently in shoebox-sized containers.

3   In school, have children look at images of work by British artist Andy Goldsworthy and have them discuss artwork ideas inspired by his work. For example, children could make spirals out of pebbles collected on the beach. Once at the beach, get them to make art by arranging natural materials in different ways. Children can also team up to make smaller installations of their own.

4   Photography is an essential component in this kind of art. After all, the art is temporary and will all be washed away by the tide. Have children and adults take photographs to record the event.

5   The Andy-Goldsworthy-inspired artwork could be integrated into a science project to make a display (see page 48). The beach could also become a focal point for the class over a number of days.

Resources
- Parents to act as helpers on the visit
- Small carrier bags
- Cameras
- Found materials
- Shoebox-sized containers

Cross-curricular links

Geography: contrast work linked to different coastal forms such as beaches, cliffs and estuaries with human intervention in the form of towns, harbours, etc.

Literacy: research and write about Andy Goldsworthy and his art. Write an imaginative adventure story which begins by finding a magical object on the beach.

Maths: children sort pebbles into different categories (size, colour etc.) and make charts to show relative numbers of each.

A sea ideas wall

This project forms an ideas wall about living by the sea – a working wall full of photos, diagrams notes, drawings, mind maps, word banks, and results of internet searches – in fact any raw material to spark imagination, creativity and motivated learning. It involves the whole school: parents, governors and the wider community. Everyone can make a contribution to the wall.

Create a community wall

Approach

1   As this is a school rather than a class project, first tell children about it in assembly. Most importantly, the wall should be divided into school house areas rather than by class, to allow children to collaborate across a range of ages.

2   To get everyone involved, write a letter to ask parents and carers to contribute photos, art, newspaper cuttings, found objects, etc.

3   Over a period of about three weeks, have children gradually create the wall. They can decide where to pin or tape their contributions. Some children may choose to make paintings at home or to write about their area in their free time.

Resources
- A large display area
- Different coloured backing paper for each school house
- Material about the community
- Sticky tape
- Staplers
- Pins

4 One of the most surprising outcomes can be the amount of historical material that may be brought in by children or loaned by adults who hear about the project. Examples may be albums of old postcards, recollections of the war or stories linked to old landmarks. It is a wonderful springboard for learning about history. Another class activity could be to map the area.

Cross-curricular links

Geography: mapping the area would be a natural follow up from the activity.

History: create a timeline for the local area. Children could also make a calendar of the main events in the community year.

Literacy: children can write about their own experiences of life in the area.

PSHE: talk about family histories and the community. The ideas wall becomes a springboard for thinking about the area and the people who live there.

A seaside village at war

Find somewhere local with historical wartime significance to visit to inspire a similar project.

A study of times past

Approach

1. Choose a historically significant place and plan a visit, e.g. a World War 2 lookout bunker.

2. In these photographs, the children met a retired soldier living in a village nearby their school. The soldier talked about the dangers of unexploded mines that can still be found on the beach and dunes nearby. Meeting a significant person allows the opportunity for discussion, e.g. the life of a soldier and what it would have been like to be posted to the lookout during wartime.

3. Get children to explore the location, making drawings and noting their feelings, impressions and questions. Use drawing boards and A3 paper so that children can work flexibly and independently. Have each child take at least one photograph.

4. Back in class, children may have many questions about the significant place. You may wish to read from a book by a local historian which describes the place of interest. The class can decide on areas for further research. At the lookout, children learned about the blackout, gas masks and what life was like for families whose loved ones were fighting overseas.

5 In their artwork, get children to explore how to combine charcoal, pen and black ink in different ways to create atmosphere. Dilute small amounts of ink to create different effects. Children can also use lines and marks in their work.

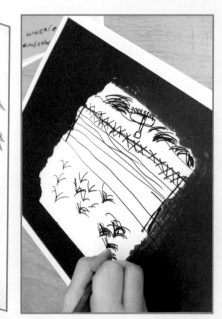

6 Photocopy and enlarge a photograph taken during the field trip. Get children to draw an imagined scene of the significant place set during wartime. Children can also make drawings of the significant place set in the present day.

7 The class could read a relevant book, for example, Michael Foreman's *War Boy: A Wartime Childhood*.

8 Use an enlarged photograph as the centre piece of the classroom display. Poems, drawings, photographs and other cross-curricular work can be added to create an atmospheric display.

Resources

- Parent helpers for visit
- A significant person
- Drawing boards
- A3 paper
- Graphic media: pens, soft drawing pencils, charcoal and black ink
- Thin and thick soft brushes for ink
- Ink containers
- Digital cameras
- Photocopier to enlarge photos to A3
- Computer, photo editing software to increase contrast and crop images

Cross-curricular links

Literacy: write about a significant place. Explore the differences between factual and imaginative writing about World War 2. Write a time-slip story about being transported into the future.

PSHE and History: ask children about family stories linked to the Second World War. Is there anything at home they could borrow to share with the class?

Our market town

This project introduces children to an art display which begins as an individual exploration and results in a collaborative display. Local markets often have historical significance and are important to the community. Many children visit the market on a weekly basis, so creating their own market stall has a particularly realistic educational value.

Begin the project by talking to children about the history of the market in your town. In the past, the castle at Tonbridge provided protection, so it was an ideal place to set up a market. This project's main aim was to get children to work in a variety of media so they could talk about texture, colour and shape. Creating vibrant textured surfaces enabled the youngest children to make visual choices as to how their creations would be displayed in the class market stall.

Creating a fruit and veg stall

Approach

1   Show children an image of a market and ask some questions about it, e.g. *What is this a picture of? Who has been to a market? What sorts of things can you buy at a market?* Show another image of a market in early England and discuss similarities and differences. *What colours, smells or sounds have you experienced in the market?*

2   Show the class a basket full of groceries. Ask the children what is in the basket and whether they know where it all comes from. Explain that all food comes from plants or animals. Find a story, song or poem which has a theme of the market or a garden.

3   Organise the class into groups, giving each a large sheet of paper. Each group will either paint, produce wax resist, collage, or use pens to draw fruit and vegetables.

4   For the wax resist group, ask children to use wax crayons (limit colours!) to cover the paper, leaving some gaps. Afterwards, another group can paint similar colours over the top in poster paint. The wax crayon will resist the paint and form an exciting texture.

5   For the collage group, again limit colours and help the children cover the paper by tearing, overlapping, or rolling tissue paper and sticking it on to create different effects.

6   Depending on the age of the class, either create thin card stencils of fruit shapes, or ask children to look at real fruit and vegetables and draw the shapes onto the underside of the pre-coloured paper. Cut out the shapes carefully.

7   Repeat these activities, rotating the class so that each child has an opportunity to use all the techniques.

8   To create a market stall, cover shoeboxes in paper or paint to look like wood. Assemble the 'produce' into the boxes, making sure they overlap to give that 'piled high' effect. Staple securely to a display board.

9   To create customers, encourage children to paint large portraits of people and fix them to the front of the stall.

10 Create a 3D canopy by bending and stapling painted cardboard to the display board and securing with staples above the boxes of produce.

11 Decorate the display with any extra touches, like flowers. Add captions with information about the market.

Resources
- Large sheets of paper
- Poster paint
- Felt-tips
- Groceries, fruit and vegetables
- Tissue paper
- Large brushes
- Wallpaper paste
- Wax crayons
- Cardboard boxes
- Staple gun (adult use only)
- Image of market

Cross-curricular links

Literacy: write a fantasy story about buying something wonderful at the market.

Maths: role play buying and selling at the market, using play money.

Science: grow your own vegetables and fruit as a class. See YouTube clips for gardening ideas.

Homes inspired by Hundertwasser

To understand the history of a local area, a great starting point is to set up a class project on children's own homes. Children usually live fairly close to the school and will have a really interesting overview of local history through the buildings they inhabit. In this project, the teacher introduces the class to an artist who uses imagery to depict the vibrancy of where we live.

This project helps children to understand when their home was built and what was going on in their local area at that time. They then create a study of their home using their research into the work of a famous Viennese artist, Friedensreich Hundertwasser.

Crazy house tiles

Approach

1 Research using books and the internet. Spend time with the class discussing Hundertwasser's work. *How does it make them feel? Can they find words to describe the paintings?*

2 In their sketchbooks, children should draw some of the shapes in the paintings, gradually building up patterns and adding colour.

3 Ask children to look at a photograph of their home and in their sketchbooks make a copy in pencil.

4 Encourage children to research the history of their home, asking parents/guardians to help in their quest.

Resources

- Examples of Hundertwasser's work
- Photographs of children's homes
- Images of Hundertwasser's paintings and buildings
- Sketchbooks
- Coloured pencils
- Air drying clay
- Acrylic paints and brushes
- PVA glue

5 At this point, children should compare the pencil sketch of their home with the buildings painted by Hundertwasser. *What do they need to add to their drawings to give them a bright and crazy style like the artist's?*

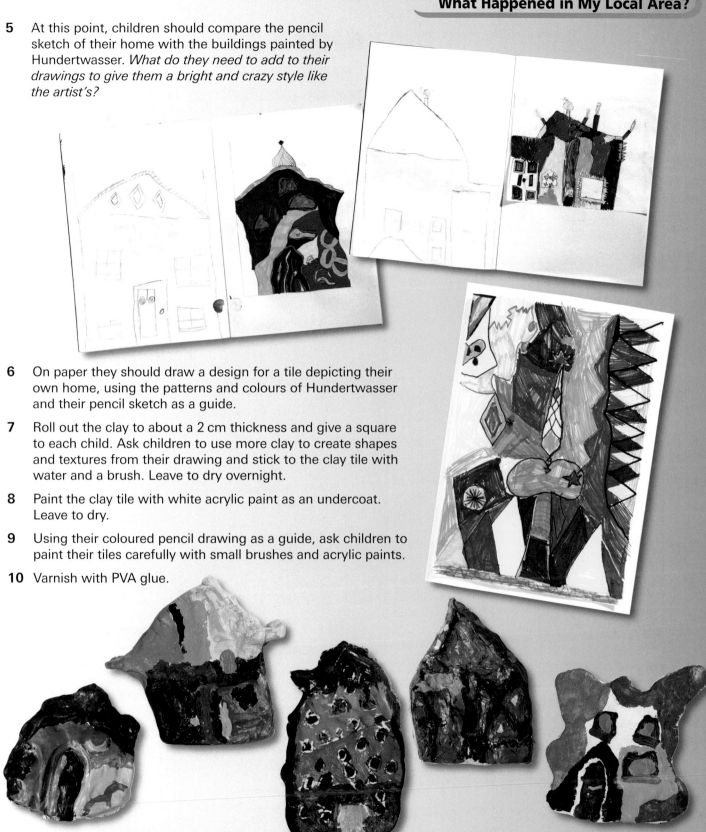

6 On paper they should draw a design for a tile depicting their own home, using the patterns and colours of Hundertwasser and their pencil sketch as a guide.

7 Roll out the clay to about a 2 cm thickness and give a square to each child. Ask children to use more clay to create shapes and textures from their drawing and stick to the clay tile with water and a brush. Leave to dry overnight.

8 Paint the clay tile with white acrylic paint as an undercoat. Leave to dry.

9 Using their coloured pencil drawing as a guide, ask children to paint their tiles carefully with small brushes and acrylic paints.

10 Varnish with PVA glue.

Cross-curricular links

Geography: use Google Earth to look at children's homes. Why were they were built in a particular area?

Literacy: ask children to write an account, real or imaginary, of someone who lived in their house before they did.

Maths: link into work based on shape and pattern.

Local memories of the Battle of Britain

I witnessed much of the Battle of Britain and I shall never forget the sight of the dog fights going on over the Weald ... and the glow in the sky as London burned during the Blitz. Later, of course, came the 'doodle bugs' which were very scary and life at school was quite different, as much of the time was spent in the shelters ... some bombs actually fell in the grounds of Tonbridge School, very close to my home.

Fredrick Morris, local resident and grandfather

There is nothing quite like hearing about actual experiences from people who saw events first-hand. In our neighbourhood, the Battle of Britain took place literally overhead and this incredible part of the Second World War is vividly remembered by elderly residents. To begin our project, it was important for children to listen and question these witnesses, who were children themselves at the time. The striking artwork of war artists CRW Nevinson and Ben Nicholson helped children understand this moment in our history.

Battle skies collage

Approach

1 Create a mixed media collage inspired by the work of war artists and the memories of local residents.

2 Ask children to start at the centre of their paper and draw a swirl in chalk pastel which expands to the outside edges.

3 Using different coloured chalks and then smudging it with their fingers, children can follow the drawn swirl to cover their paper with colours, creating the impression of an explosion.

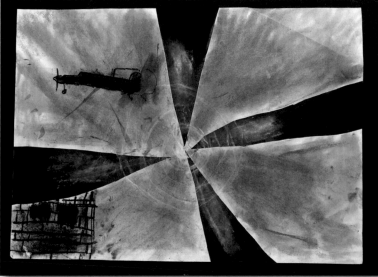

4 Now cut a whole sheet of black sugar paper into triangles. (These do not need to be even.) Get children to match up these triangles at the corners of their chalk drawings and stick them down.

5 Cut out warplane silhouettes and ask children to stick these into the gaps on their composition.

6 Add some chalk over the collage and smudge it in with your fingers to evoke a sense of movement and space.

Resources
- A3 paper
- Chalk pastels
- Black sugar paper
- Images of war planes
- Glue

Aeroplane sculptures

Approach

1   Study the painting 'Dead Sea' by war artist Paul Nash. Children can then design and construct a 3D crashed plane using basic shapes to form the structure.

2   In their sketchbooks, ask children to draw or collage simple shapes to create a design for the structure of their plane sculpture.

3   They can then copy the shapes onto thin card and cut them out with scissors.

4   Spend some time helping the children to staple their cardboard shapes securely to the hardboard. Once they are happy with this, they should bend and fold their constructions into the desired design, strengthening the whole structure with masking tape.

5   Layer strips of wet Modroc over the whole structure, working from the bottom up to prevent it collapsing.

6   Leave the planes to dry and paint them with acrylic colours.

7   Children can add extra details and varnish with a coat of PVA glue.

Resources

- Sketchbooks
- Pencils and collage papers
- Thin cardboard
- Scissors
- Masking tape
- Staple guns (adult use only)
- Sheets of hardboard for the base
- Modroc
- Acrylic paint
- PVA glue

Further ideas

Instead of making a 3D sculpture, cut shapes out of different coloured sugar paper and use charcoal to add shadow and light.

Cross-curricular links

History: start a project based on recollections of local people about major events and the effect on the community. How was the local area affected by war?

Literacy: look at some creative writing influenced by the war poets. Write an imaginative account of an air battle during World War 2.

A royal connection

Many places have a variety of royal connections. For example, during Tudor times during Tudor times, Tonbridge had a population of 500 people, but it was visited regularly by both Henry VIII and Elizabeth I. This project gives an opportunity for exciting cross-curricular work in art and history. Children can produce beautiful Tudor- style portraits while learning about the customs, costume and society of Tudor Tonbridge.

A Tudor portrait gallery

Approach

1 Explain that a portrait was an important symbol of wealth and status for the Tudors. In an age without newspapers or photography, portrait painters were the paparazzi of their time. This project emphasises the importance of the painting process: from learning about drawing proportions to embellishing with jewels. A satisfying finished image needs careful planning.

2 Start by looking at Tudor portraits. You may find good examples at local galleries or historic houses. You will also find Tudor portraits online at the National Portrait Gallery, Tate Britain and a range of history websites.

3 Ask children to look at how Tudor portraits are composed. Look at what kinds of backgrounds are used, the facial expressions of the sitters, how textiles and jewels are presented, and what kind of frames the pictures had. Encourage children to make notes and sketches. Discuss the proportions of a face and its relation to the body. Children can try 'measuring' their face with their hand.

4   Ask children to choose their favourite Tudor. On a piece of thick drawing paper, encourage them to draw the outline of the face lightly with pencil, remembering what they have discovered about proportions.

5   *Which colours need to be mixed to create a skin tone?* Demonstrate children's suggestions and talk about what else they may need.

6   Show children how to use a brush carefully: mixing the colours in the palette with a clean brush, making sure they are not using too much water on the brush and not painting next to a different colour while it is still wet, etc.

7   Give the children a range of collage materials to stick on their painting. Discuss the materials and show them images of the type of fabrics and jewellery the Tudors wore.

8   Make a frame from strips of card stuck together and decorate with collaged patterns, before painting with gold paint.

9   Put the portrait in the frame and glue in place. Display the portraits as a 'gallery' together with written work about each chosen Tudor.

Further ideas

The Tudors played some of the same games we play today, such as draughts and cards. Ask children to create a board game and work out the rules. You could call it 'Tudor pursuits' and base it on facts about the Tudors.

Look at Tudor portraits and design a Tudor costume, using collage sequins for an ornate effect. Personalise the costume by cutting a hole for the child's own face.

Resources

- Pencils
- Thick paper
- Scissors
- Watercolour paints
- Thick and thin paint brushes for backgrounds and fine detail
- Palettes and water pots
- Collage materials
- Card
- Gold poster paint
- PVA glue
- Scissors

Cross-curricular links

History: research your own Tudor banquet.

Literacy: write a letter from Anne Boleyn to Henry VIII from the Tower.

PE: research some of the early games the Tudors played, like football, hockey and tennis, and play your own versions of them.

Science: explore the history of paints. What can you use to make colours?

Neighbourhood wish tree

The starting point for this project was a piece of interactive street art designed by Yoko Ono. Her 'Wish Tree' consisted of hundreds of parcel labels, each with a wish written on it, suspended from a living tree. The general public were encouraged to interact with the art by reading the wishes and then adding their own and tying the label to the tree. The wishes themselves are often thought-provoking and moving.

Wish tree

Approach

1   Ask children to investigate different ways of recording and symbolising hopes and wishes for their future, their community and the wider world.

2   Introduce children to Yoko Ono's wish tree concept.

3   Give every child in the school a parcel tag and invite them to write a wish for their local community. Children can decorate the reverse side if desired.

4   Encourage interaction with the finished work by leaving a small pile of tags and pens for children, parents, teachers and school visitors to leave their own wishes.

Resources
● Parcel tags
● String

Collage tree on canvas

Approach

1 Discuss the importance of trees in our neighbourhood. Talk about their physical characteristics and how they make us feel. If possible, visit a local park with the children and choose a tree for the class to depict in a collaborative collage.

2 Prepare a canvas by doing a blue and green wash in the background.

3 Paint the trunk and main branches of the tree.

4 Provide the children with a range of types and colours of paper to choose from and ask each child to cut out and decorate a leaf.

5 Invite children to stick leaves to the tree using PVA glue.

Further ideas

Create a display of mini-wish trees. Get children to write their wish on a small piece of paper and place in a small red envelope. Make the mini-wish trees by binding small branches together with colourful string and attach to a display board. Tie string off each of the branches and staple the red envelopes to the string. Decorate with glitter, paint or scrap materials.

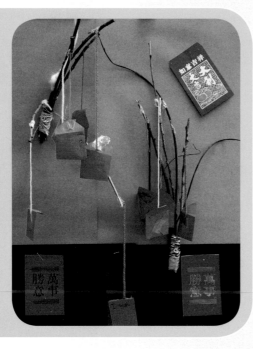

Resources

- Large square canvas
- Watercolour or poster paints
- A range of paper types and colours
- Scissors
- Pencils, pens and crayons in a variety of colours

Cross-curricular links

Literacy: write formal letters requesting action on local issues.

RE: investigate the importance of prayer in different religions, and look at traditions linked to personal improvement and self-control such as Lent and Ramadam.

Science: research trees as recyclers of carbon dioxide, investigate the seasons, and the life cycles of plants.

Hempen homespuns

In this project, children can investigate how various fabrics and threads could be recycled and reused. The term 'hempen homespuns' arose from Shakespeare's 'A Midsummer Night's Dream' and was used by the fairies to describe the workmen in the woods (one of whom was, of course, a weaver). From this, the importance of cloth and weaving can be discussed and the complex processes that go into the manufacture of apparently simple garments can be explained. (*Have you ever tried making a t-shirt starting with a reel of cotton?*) In advance of this project, ask children to collect scraps of fabrics.

Weaving using recycled fabrics

Approach

1   Invite children to look at how old fabric and thread can be reused. Encourage them to look at examples of this from around the world. You could even invite someone from another country into the school to talk about how materials are recycled in another country.

2   Prepare looms for children from recycled card by cutting 'v' grooves into the card at 1.5 cm intervals at either end. If using corrugated card, widen the warp in the same direction as the card corrugations.

3   Show children how to tether the warp thread to a punched hole near one end, wind the warp thread around the grooves and tie off at the diagonally opposite end on another hole.

4   It is important that once the children are familiar with this basic set-up that they are given the opportunity to experiment with different arrangements of the materials. For example what effect does spacing out the warp threads have (say from 1.5 cm to 3 cm)? Or what is the effect of using different threads for the warp – for example, polyester and nylon threads are quite slippery and this can result in the weft working its way loose. Children can once again investigate different strategies to overcome these problems.

5   Ask children to prepare strips of material for weaving. They can experiment with different fabrics and ways of making thin strips. Some fabric tears easily whereas other will need to be cut with scissors. Alternative materials can be introduced such as ribbon, wool, string and even paper.

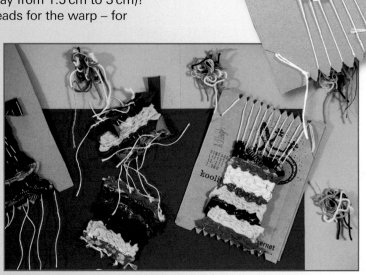

6   Weave into the weft threads by threading a strip of material over and under the warp threads in one direction. Turn around when you reach the end of the line of warp threads. Take care not to over-tighten and narrow the resulting rug. The start and end of the threads are simply tucked in.

7   As rows are completed, a fork can be used to comb down the weft, although with coarse weft threads and widely spaced warp, little fingers do a much better job!

8   When the weaving is complete the warp threads are cut on the back of the loom leaving plenty of room for tying off by knotting adjacent pairs of warp threads close to the top or bottom of the rug.

9   Finished work can then be used as place mats.

Resources

- Scraps of fabric at least 0.5 m long
- Card
- Scissors
- Warp thread

Further ideas

- Create a large-scale rug as a class or whole school.
- Create pictures or moods with the rugs by carefully selecting colours and textures and placing them on the work.

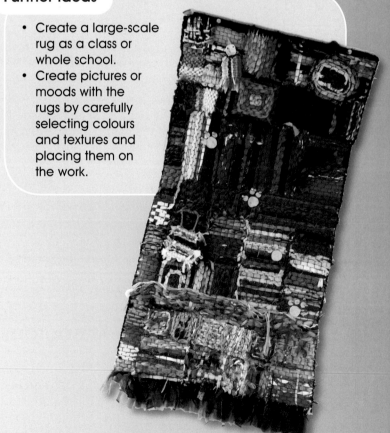

Cross-curricular links

History: research the mechanisation of spinning and weaving and create a time line to record the developments.

Literacy: discuss myths related to weaving, e.g. Arachne.

Science: test a variety of fabrics for strength and water resistance.

Games from rubbish

The starting point for this project was the idea of making toys from found or recycled materials. There are many examples of this from history and from other cultures. These include the idea of 'make do and mend', which is often considered when studying Second-World-War-based topics or simple traditional toys in topics on the Victorians. For this topic, the children were inspired by creative and inventive work of contemporary Nigerian children who make toys from a range of recycled and found materials.

Games from recycled materials

Approach
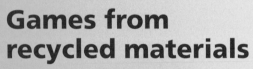

1 Introduce children to a number of toys made from recycled materials, including vehicles, musical instruments, figures and simple games. Look at examples and discuss the aesthetic qualities of the materials used to make them. For example, *why would a piece of driftwood generally be considered more pleasing than a similar-sized piece of wood freshly cut from a length of new timber?*

2 Ask children to think about a toy that they would like to make from a selection shown to them, and come up with initial ideas on how to proceed with the materials available. This will often mean their ideas will need to be modified or even abandoned if suitable materials are not available.

3 Demonstrate a few simple techniques for joining materials and safe methods for making holes in materials before getting children to start making their toy. Develop their ideas as they go, testing, and changing things if required. It is a good idea for adults to drill or punch a hole into bottle tops in advance, making sure there are no sharp edges.

4 Allow children to follow their own ideas and to solve problems themselves rather than follow a set of instructions. With perseverance, children will often come up with innovative and appropriate solutions to the problems they encounter. For example, one child making a toy guitar found that the strings distorted the cardboard and found a way to reinforce the cardboard with lollisticks glued on the back.

Resources
- Plastic screw-type bottle and carton lids
- Reclaimed wood (driftwood if possible)
- Stones and pebbles
- Plastic bottles
- String and thread
- Sticks and twigs
- Cardboard food boxes
- Wire – florist or thin garden
- Lollisticks
- Other suitable recycled or found materials
- PVA glue
- Blue tack
- Holepunch

Further ideas

Shakers:
Shakers can be made from materials such as holed bottle tops or bottle caps threaded onto garden wire and secured to a handle. The handle can be decorated with coloured threads, etc. Alternatively, a cardboard or plastic tube can be part-filled with grains and sealed, then similarly decorated.

Vehicles:
Plastic bottles and cardboard boxes make an ideal chassis but holes will need to be carefully made in which to insert axles made from sticks or straws. Wheels can be made from bottle tops or carefully cut from card. Adding ballast in the form of pebbles or stones helps the vehicle to remain upright and will also help the wheels to rotate when pulled.

Strategy games:
Bottle tops secured to a base made from recycled wood or driftwood make attractive grids for games like noughts and crosses or draughts. Playing pieces can be made from attractive pebbles or stones.

Cross-curricular links

Art: create a display board with children's illustrations of their lunchtime play activities. Have children draw themselves playing sport or using the play equipment and attach it to a schoolyard background.

History: create timelines of popular children's games.

Literacy: write instructions for making a 'found materials' toy.

Music: create musical instruments using waste materials.

Science: research biodegradable and non-biodegradable materials.

Recycling your rubbish

The starting point for this project was the idea of the places we need to travel to recycle waste. This geography-based project was aimed at giving the children a better understanding of the facilities available in their local community. In this project, recycling was the chosen theme, but the study would have worked equally well with other community facilities that children care about and use such as sports facilities, shops and clubs.

Recycling map

Approach

1   Ask children to list all the things that can be recycled in their community. In our class some children were surprised that shoes, batteries and books could be recycled and that organised recycling went beyond materials such as glass, paper and tin cans that are more commonly collected at the road side.

2   Show children a map of the local area. Work together to mark a number of known recycling locations on it.

3   Organise a walk so the children can visit these sites. Ask them to record exactly what could be recycled and how far they had to walk to get there.

4   Look at maps with the collected information. Children will now have a much better sense of scale and be able to make much better judgements relating to how easy these recycling points are to reach.

5   Provide children with a simplified map of their town. This can be created by tracing over a published map and marking key streets and buildings.

Resources
- Simplified maps of the local area/town
- Tracing paper
- Coloured pens/pencils
- String or thread

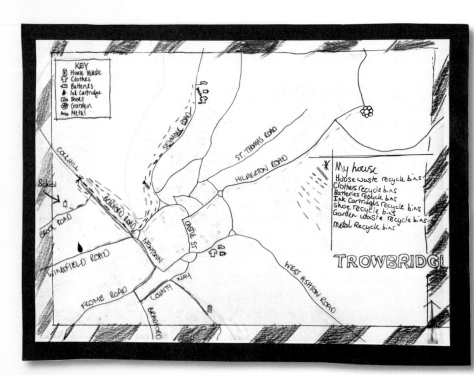

6 Ask children to mark all the places they had found for recycling. Encourage them to look at the graphics created for published maps before designing their own symbols to indicate these places. Any further recycling locations that were revealed through further research should also be marked on the map.

7 Ask children to mark the location of their own home on their map (or the school location if they did not live close enough) and then draw colour-coded lines to indicate the routes they could take from their homes to reach these facilities.

Further ideas

Mark circles indicating 'as the crow flies' distances from the recycling facilities on children's maps. Use colour coding and a key to represent distance.

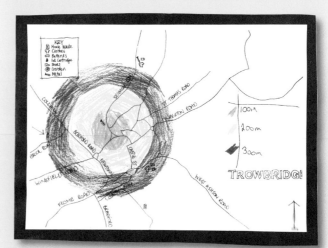

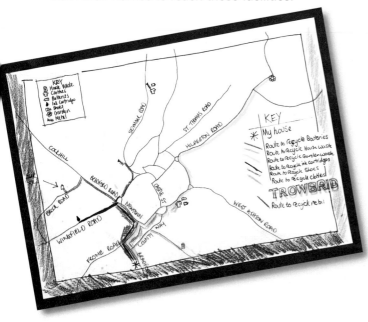

8 Show children how to approximate a journey distance by using a piece of string placed along the route and then holding the string against a scale appropriate for the map.

9 Display maps together on a colourful background with a clear title.

Write letters to the town council summarising the findings and requesting that additional facilities be provided in areas of the town where provision was poor.

Take on the role of town planner. Ask children to collate results in order to look for trends and patterns. Children may notice that a particular area is either very well or very poorly served with recycling facilities generally, or for a particular material. Discuss the sorts of strategic decisions that need to be taken by local authorities when deciding on the type and location of facilities in their communities. For example, children will often complain that there are no parks near their home or that they have to travel across town to reach a dance class or swimming club.

Cross-curricular links

Art and Design: design logos or map key symbols for recycling materials.

Geography: make posters explaining the differences between degradable and non-degradeable materials.

History: research the history of rubbish disposal – bottle tips, rag and bones, dust carts.

Literacy: write the 'life stories' of recycleable materials.